THE
UNBELIEVABLE
TRUTH

THE
UNBELIEVABLE

My Personal Walk With God

Pastor Emerson D. Broadnax

ARPress
ILLUMINATING IDEAS.
EMPOWERING VOICES

ARPress

45 Dan Road Suite 5

Canton MA 02021

Hotline:	1(888) 821-0229
Fax:	1(508) 545-7580

Ordering Information:

Quantity sales. Special discounts are available on quantity purchases by corporations, associations, and others. For details, contact the publisher at the address above.

Printed in the United States of America.

ISBN-13:	Paperback	979-8-89356-834-9
	eBook	979-8-89356-835-6
	Hardback	979-8-89356-836-3

Library of Congress Control Number: 2024908963

Table of Contents

Dedication

This is dedicated to God, who is the head of my life. To my Parents the Late Charles and Georgia Broadnax who The Lord used to bring me into this world and to the late Bishop Kenneth H. Moales, Sr., who helped me to become the holy man of God that I am today.

David said:

Let the redeemed of the Lord say so whom the Lord hath redeemed out of the hand of the enemy.

For He brought me out of the horrible pit, out of the miry clay, and set my feet upon a rock and established my goings, and hath put a new song in my mouth, even praise unto our God: many shall see it, and fear, and shall trust in the Lord.

(Psalms 107:1-2 and 40:2-3)

This book is about how God delivered me out of a twenty-nine-year drug habit and how I have been free for twenty-four years. It is about the various ways He has manifested himself to me over the years; saving, delivering and healing me. It's about the Lord speaking to me in an audible voice in dreams and visions and through Bishop Moales. and other people and most importantly through His word. It is about God making me a prophet, minister and pastor. It is about me being attacked by demonic spirits on several occasions.

2nd Corinthians 5:17

Galatians 1:1

St. John 15:16

St. Luke 10:19

1st John 4: 11

St. Mark 16: 17-18

Foreword I

Psalm 37:23, "The steps of a good man are ordered by the Lord, and he delighted in His way."

Elder Emerson Broadnax wrote this biography to encourage others to walk in the steps that the Lord has ordered for them. It does not matter whether they are men or women, young or old; the steps are yet in place. The sequence of events is real and the way each of the steps is explained is so simple that a wayfaring stranger could not go wrong.

This book is now giving a written testimony to many about the life of one who found that God is real. Elder Broadnax accepted him as a person that walked in the steps that God had ordered for him. He found that the steps continued as he followed them. The accounts of his life are real and the changes became easier as he walked in the footsteps that God had ordered for him.

Father Stanley Arrington, Cathedral of the Holy Spirit

Foreword II

A thought provoking, inspirational, comfortable and easy read. This testimony is heartfelt and personal. The author's experiences feel real and speak to his deep faith and trust in the spiritual heavens. May we all develop the kind of peace that comes with a true understanding of what it means when we believe that God is our friend and Savior who is truly here to take care of us. Thank you for sharing and spreading this trust and uplifting belief in God's love.

Your friend, C. Alexis

Foreword III

Emerson: 9/13/92

Remember Ps. 24:4, "One thing that I have desired of the Lord, that will I seek after; that I may dwell in the house of the Lord all the days of my life, to behold the beauty of the Lord, and to inquire in his temple."

"Remember to thine ownself be true, then thou canst not be false to any man." — Shakespeare

Thank the Lord for your spiritual growth since the ninety and nine that Friday night witness. The word of God will always be your rule and measure. The Holy Ghost will reveal God in you. You are a spiritual son in the faith. God has great plans for you. Be faithful!

Pastor Moales

(The Late Bishop Kenneth H. Moales)

Preface

I call this book *The Unbelievable Truth* because some of these stories seem unbelievable. Nevertheless, they are true. I would dare not lie about God or on God. In this day of unbelief, people need to know that God is real and that he is yet moving by his spirit.

Paul says in Galatians 1:20, "Before God I lie not." John says in Revelation 21:8, "All liars shall have their part in the lake of fire and brimstone which is the second death."

Numbers 23:19, "God is not a man that he should lie; nor the Son of man that he should repent, hath he not said it? And shall he not do it, or hath he not spoken it? And shall he not make it good."

Isaiah 40:8, "For the grass withereth and the flower fadeth; but the word of God shall stand forever!"

Amen.

Elder Emerson Broadnax

Introduction

"The Unbelievable Truth"

I left work one Friday evening to go home, not knowing that later on that night my life would change forever. I had promised myself during the week that I was not going to get high like I had done so many times before. However, as soon as I got to my side of town I went into the liquor store and brought some rum and coke and a Budweiser beer.

After drinking I decided that I wanted to get some cocaine, so I went up the street and found that someone in Tiffany's Café was selling the drug. I went to the café, but prior to going in I set my Budweiser on the side of the building and went inside to buy the cocaine. As I exited Tiffany's, I retrieved my beer and headed home.

A group of people from the church stopped and asked me if they could speak with me. I immediately said yes and listened to what they had to say. After talking to me for a while they asked me if I wanted to be saved. I said yes and they told me to recite the Sinner's Prayer of Salvation. I asked them if I needed to put my Budweiser down and they said no. I recited the Sinner's Prayer and they talked to me some more about God. I then promised them that I would attend their church. I went home and shot the cocaine and continued getting high. As I continued to get high, I decided that I would take them up on their offer and go to their church and seek more help from God. I knew that I could not live the way that I was living.

I knew that if I did not stop doing drugs that I would end up dead or incarcerated. I knew that I needed help and I believed that God could help me. One night I was in the room trying to get high, and I heard a song by Michael Jackson on the radio. "I am looking at the man in the mirror; I'm asking him to change his ways." By hearing this song that was playing I decided that I would go to church that Sunday, which happened to be my birthday.

From that moment on I promised myself that I would go every Sunday and I did. No matter what I was going through during the course of the week, I was at church on Sunday. When I found out that there was a midweek service I would attend that service as well. The more I heard the word and went to church, the more I believed that I could be saved and delivered.

Oftentimes I would arrive to church early but there was no one there. I would sit on the steps and wait patiently for someone to come and open the church. One day Bishop Moales said that he was going to give me a key to the church. He said that if no one was at the church on time he knew that I would be and, as promised, he gave me a key.

Over the course of a year and one half, God delivered me from a twenty- three year drug habit and I have been clean and free ever since. God has continuously been manifesting himself in my life since that day.

Psalm 10 7:2

Psalm 23:3

Psalm 40:1-2

St. John 8:36

2nd Corinthians 5:17

Galatians 1:4

Chapter 1

The Voice Of God

"And the Lord God called unto Adam and said unto Him, Where art thou?" Genesis 3:9

"And when the Lord saw that he turned aside to see God called unto him in the midst of the bush and said Moses, Moses and He said here I am." Exodus 3:4

"And Jesus when He was baptized went up straightway out of the water; and low the heavens were opened unto Him, and He saw the Spirit of God descending like a dove and lightning upon him: and lo a voice from heaven saying, This is my beloved Son in whom I am well pleased." St. Matthew 3: 16-17

"And as He journeyed He came near to Damascus and suddenly there shined round about him a light from heaven. And He fell to the earth, and heard a voice saying unto him Saul, Saul why persecutest thou me." Acts 9:3- 4

These following chapters are about how God has manifested himself to me over the years. They are about

Him speaking to me in an audible voice, dreams, and visions. They speak about healing, demonic spirits, and what people have said to me about my spiritual walk with God.

That's Just Not True

A Poem by Elder Emerson Broadnax

The fool hath said in his heart that there is no God, but that's just not true!

For God is my deliverer, He's the one who brought me through.

He's my Alpha and Omega, my beginning and my end!

He's not only my Lord and Savior; but He's also my friend.

And what He has done for me He will also do for you.

But you must have faith and trust for Him to see you through He's the God of all flesh and all power is in his hands.

He created the little children, He created the woman and the man.

So listen up my friend, to what I am telling you.

For when they say that there is no God, my friend that's just not true!

Psalm14:1

Psalm 24:1

St. John 3:16-17

1st John 3:8

Galatians 1:4

Genesis House

I was living at Genesis House for a few months when God spoke to me in a dream. He said, "You are my prophet," and in the dream I replied, "No, I am not." God spoke to me again in a deep, stern voice and said, "You are my prophet." I sat up in the bed and said, "Yes, Lord." I began to shake and looked around the room. I told God that I was not a prophet because I was not fully delivered and did not know or understand the meaning of a prophet. I did not realize that God had a plan and purpose for my life (Psalm 23:3, Psalm 40:2, 2nd Corinthians 5:17, Galatians 1:1). God has been manifesting himself to me in various ways from that moment on.

Praising God

I was in church one night and the people were praising and worshipping God. I was also praising God but felt bound. I was struggling because many things in my life were not right. When we stopped praising God and sat down I heard a voice say to me, "Anybody can praise me when things are going good, but it takes a good man to praise me when things are not as good.' As I sat in the first pew I turned around to see who was talking to me. I looked in front and behind me and no one was there. I then looked up in the air and stopped and caught myself as I did not want anyone to think that I was crazy or losing my mind.

All Night Prayer

The church was having all night prayer from 12:00 midnight to 6:00 in the morning. I was lying down, hoping that I would get up by 11:30 p.m. so that I would make it to prayer, but I overslept. In spite of getting up late I made it to prayer by 3:00 and was glad that I did, even though I was late. I got down on my knees to pray and I heard a still, quiet voice say that we have saints, haints and ain'ts in the church. I said to myself: *Why are you having these thoughts and thinking something like that?* I asked my pastor about the thought that I was having and he said that we have saints, haints and ain'ts in the church. Bishop Moales said the saints were the ones that were there to do the will of God, the haints were the ones that were there to hinder the will of God, and the ain'ts were the ones that were just there. He said that people were going to do whatever they wanted, one way or another.

The Switch is Off

It was very cold in the church where we were having all night prayer. As I was praying I heard a quiet, still voice say, "The switch is off." I said to myself, *I am not going to say anything to anyone because they are going to think that I am losing my mind.* The next day I heard them say that the furnace repairman was there and he said, "The switch is off."

The Door is not Locked

One day I was in Carter's Barber Shop. Mr. Carter was in the hospital; therefore, I had to wait for his daughter to cut my hair. I waited for her to cut my hair and stayed around the shop until closing. As we exited out of the barbershop she placed the padlock on the door, we said our good-byes and she drove off. I lived about a block from the shop, and as I got halfway to my house I kept hearing a voice say, "The door is not locked." I kept walking and continued to hear the voice say, "The door is not locked." I said to myself, *I am not going back to the shop as they might think that I am trying to break in.* I continued to make my way home and once in my house I went upstairs to my bedroom. Again I heard the voice say, "The door is not locked," and I once again said that I was not going back to the shop. However, the voice would not leave and I found myself walking in circles in my kitchen. I said to myself, *let me go back*, which I did. I ran into Mrs. Blackwell who asked, "Where are you going"? I responded that I was going to the barber shop because the door was not locked.

The words just rolled off my tongue without me realizing it. Mrs. Blackwell said, "What do you mean, 'The door is not locked'?"

I said, "Yes, the Lord spoke to me and told me that the door is not locked." She gave me a strange look and as we approached the front door of the shop I noticed a big padlock on the door. I said, "This is not the one." There were two more doors, one on the right side and one on the left. I went over to the right side and looked and said, "That is not the one." She was looking at me strangely. We then walked around to the left side and I said, "That is the one." I turned the knob and the door flew wide open. Mrs. Blackwell asked me again as she stood standing with her eyes wide open as big as marbles. I responded the Lord told me the door was not locked. There was a gentleman who lived in the upstairs apartment that was able to gain entry to the barbershop from inside and was able to lock the door, making sure everything was safe.

This is not Acceptable to God

One Sunday morning I was attending the church service when the praise and worship team was leading the congregation in song. I thought to myself, *this is not acceptable to God*. I then said to myself, *why are you being judgmental?* Meanwhile, the late Bishop Kenneth H. Moales came down from his office and began to sing an old hymn. He led the praise and worship team and at the end he turned around and said, "I don't know what you were doing and singing, but that was not acceptable to God." Once again I realized that the Lord was speaking to me.

I Wonder Who is Preaching Tomorrow

We were having services all weekend in Hartford, CT. I was sitting in my car in the church parking lot, waiting for the bus to take us to Hartford. I was wondering to myself, *who is preaching at our church in the morning?* I heard a voice in the spirit say, "You are." The bus arrived, I boarded and we were on our way to Hartford. As I was sitting in the stand during service, I saw Bishop Moales call his attendant, Deacon Mark Brevard, over to him and I noticed that they were both looking at me.

When the service was over and I was getting ready to go to the bus, Deacon Mark Brevard suddenly approached me and said, "Bishop wants to see you."

As I made my way to Bishop, I passed Lady Moales who stated, "I was wondering who was going to preach at the church tomorrow and the Lord told me *you*."

When I reached Bishop he said, "I want you to preach at the church tomorrow."

I said, "Yes, Bishop," and walked away.

As I boarded the bus to head back to Bridgeport, I saw Mother Braxton sitting in the first row of the bus. She said unto me, "I wondered who was preaching at the church in the morning and the spirit said *you*!"

Yesterday, Today and Tomorrow

Yesterday is dead and gone! All I have is today and tomorrow. All I have is today and my memories of yesterday. All I have is today and my hopes and aspirations for today and tomorrow!

Philippians 3:13

Hebrews 11:1

St. Mark 9:23

Chapter 2

Dreams And Visions

"For God speaketh once, yea twice, yet man perceiveth it not in a dream, in a vision of the night, when deep sleep falleth upon men in slumbering upon the bed; then he open the ears of men and sealeth their instruction; that he may withdraw men from their purpose and hold pride from man." Job 33:14- 17

"And Joseph dreamed a dream, and he told it to his brethren: and they hated him yet the more." Genesis 37:5

"But while he thought on those things, behold the angel of the Lord appeared unto him in a dream, saying Joseph thou son of David, fear not to take unto thee Mary thy wife: for that which I have conceived in her is of the Holy Ghost." Matthew 1:20

"And there was a certain disciple at Damascus, named Ananias; and to him said the Lord in a vision Ananias. And he said behold, I am here Lord." Acts 9:10

You Know You are a Minister

In this particular dream I was walking down State Street in Bridgeport, CT. In the dream there was a gentleman on the roof of a house with his son. He began jabbing at me with a very long stick and then he chased me down State Street with a two by four slab of wood, "You know you are a minister." This was the fourth or fifth dream I had concerning myself becoming a minister. I went to my pastor, Bishop Moales and said "Pastor, I believe God has a calling on my life."

Bishop's reply was, "I will put you up and let you speak, at which time I will know if this is true or not." I then preached and Bishop said, "Yes, God has placed a calling on your life."

Pastor, the Phone is for You

I had a dream that I was walking down Connecticut Avenue, in Bridgeport CT near Hollister Avenue. As I walked down the street there was a pay phone ringing nearby. There was an unidentified man that answered the phone. He took the phone and handed it over to me and said, "Pastor, the phone is for you." So I went over and answered the call.

Lady in Arguments

I had a dream about a lady in our church on three separate occasions. In my dream she was in an argument with another woman. On this particular Saturday, she walked in while I was working in the feeding program.

I said to myself, *God has delivered her into my hands; therefore, I had better mention the dreams that I have had.* The woman started to leave when I called after her. She said to me, "Just because you don't have a title does not mean that I can't receive a word from you." I told her about the dreams that I was having and she confirmed that she had been having an issue with this particular woman. She indicated that she had had enough and was about to lose her religion. The woman realized that the Lord was speaking to her through me and she decided to go home instead of seeking out the woman to settle their differences.

Why Are You Acting Like That?

In my dream I saw a young girl at my church. God had spoken to her and said that he did not know why she was acting this way when her parents raised her to be better than that. When I saw the young lady I told her about the dream that I had; however, she never responded. I found out later that the young girl's parents were both ministers and her grandfather was a bishop.

Wife is Pregnant

I had a dream that a young man named Shamar Young's wife was about three or four months pregnant. When I saw him I asked if she was pregnant and he said he did not know. Shamar said that his wife had been getting sick lately and they were going to visit the doctor that day. I saw him a week later with a big smile on his face. He yelled, "You were right! You were right! My wife is four months pregnant."

The House Deal

I dreamed that a deacon in my church was going to purchase a home. In the dream the Lord showed me that the realtor was trying to swindle the deacon out of his money. I called the deacon and told him about my dream. He said that he was going to close the deal with him; however, due to the revelation of my dream there would be no deal.

Young Woman Minister

I had a dream about a young woman minister in my church. In my dream, God said, "All things work for the good of all who love him; and are called according to his purpose." When I saw her I told her and she burst into tears. She said, "You just don't understand. I go around preaching to others, people are being healed, delivered and set free and I am all alone."

"But God was saying you are not alone. I know how you feel and all things are working for your good."

Miracles in Jesus' Name

I dreamed that a minister was in my basement praying over the house. When I saw him I asked if he would come and pray a blessing over my house and he said that he would. After service one Sunday morning he affirmed that he would come to my house and pray. He wanted to know why I was so adamant about him praying over my house when he was not a member of the church (and there were over thirty ministers at the church at the time). I explained that he was the person that the Lord showed me in the dream. He came over to my house and went into the basement to the very spot where I saw him praying in my dream. He grabbed my hands and began to pray. When he finished praying he said, "Emerson, I saw you working miracles in Jesus' Name."

God is Showing You Hell

I was walking down the street near Braxton's men's clothing store on Stratford Avenue. I saw men working in the manhole nearby. As a young child I was always fearful of manholes. However, in my dream I went over and looked down into it, watching the men at work. As I peered down deeper I saw a canyon that went down Stratford Avenue to St. Michael's Cemetery (about fourteen blocks). The canyon looked like burning rocks that were bright purple, yellow, red and orange in color. I asked Bishop Moales about my dream and he told me that God was showing me hell. I had another dream six months later and in the dream the canyon had widened to include Orange Street. I told Bishop once again and he responded that hell was enlarging itself.

The Newspaper

One night I had a dream that there was a big article in the paper about my pastor. That evening after work I was going into prayer and my pastor was coming out. I asked him if I could speak to him for a minute and he said yes. I told him that I had a dream about him that night and there was a big newspaper article about him. He looked at me and smiled and said that he was called at 12:00 that afternoon and was told that they were going to do an article on him.

"Jesus Wants to Take You to the Promised Land" Poem by Elder Emerson Broadnax

Don't let the problems of the world slowly get you down
Remember Jesus is our Savior; He's always around.

He died on the cross one sad and lonely day

But remember when He died, He washed our sins away.
So don't get discouraged when the devil comes around
Because Jesus gave his promise to never let us down.

Love is the key to the problems of the world

Yes, love is the key for man and woman, boy and girl.
Open up your heart and let love shine through

And surely, you will see there is no need to be blue.

Jesus has shown his light on me; it can happen to you
Just have faith and trust; that's all you've got to do.

So, don't let the devil lead you astray

And surely, you will be rewarded on Judgment Day.

The door is open; He's waiting just for you
He wants to take us to the Promised Land
Like He said He would do.

John 10:10-11

John 14:1

John 14:6

Healing

"I am the Lord thy God that healeth thee." Exodus 15:26

"Who forgiveth all thine iniquities, who healeth all thy diseases." Psalm 103:3

"The writing of Hezekiah King of Judah, when he had been sick, and was recovered of his sickness." Isaiah 38:9

"Verily, verily, I say unto you, He that believeth on me, the works that I do, shall he do also, and greater works that these shall he do, because I go unto my father." St. John 14:12

"And these signs shall follow thee that believe. In my name they shall cast out devils; they shall speak with new tongues; They shall take up serpents; and if they drink any deadly thing, it shall not hurt them, they shall lay hands on the sick and they shall recover." St. Mark 16:17-18

"And the Lord wrought special miracles by the Lord of Paul." Acts 19:11

Lobster Bisque Soup

One day I was at work and the owner said she was going down the street to get lunch, so I asked her if she could buy me some lobster bisque soup. When she came back with the soup I started eating it as I continued working. We had a lot of work to do, so I was eating and working at the same time. As I was working I had a vision in my head of me breaking out in bumps; I ignored it and kept on working. I began to feel very hot and went to the bathroom to splash water on my face. As I began doing so I started to see myself breaking out in bumps, and I said, "Oh, no." I kept splashing water on my face and the bumps were getting worse, and started to connect. Some of them looked like whelps. I could feel them on the bottoms of my feet. The whelps were so bad it made me look like Linda Blair, from the *Exorcist* movie.

I went to sit down and my boss was hysterical. She wanted to take me to the hospital, but I refused to go. She said she was going to the drug store to get an antibiotic. While she was gone I began to drink some water and began reading my prayer book. The fervent, effective prayer of a righteous man availeth much (James 5:16). As I read these prayers aloud to myself I felt a burning sensation going on in my stomach.

When my boss came back with the antibiotic I took a pill to satisfy her but I was already feeling better. She told me that I could go home, so I went out to catch the bus and waited. As I waited I felt as if I was going to pass out. I then looked up to heaven and cried out, "Jesus!" Instantly, I began to feel better. As the bus pulled up I climbed aboard and took a seat in the back. I was feeling self-conscious because the bumps were still visible. When I got home I went straight to bed and when I woke up it was as if nothing had ever happened.

Nursing Home

I was in the nursing home on Bond Street, in Bridgeport, CT where we were having church service. One of the church members had taken ill and had to be transported to St. Vincent's hospital. When I went to see her she was not conscious. I did not know if she was heavily sedated or asleep. She was hooked up to a lot of machines; therefore, I sat there, prayed for her and left the room. A few days later I returned to the hospital and again she was unconscious or asleep. Once again I prayed for her and left. I came back a couple of days later to visit her and she was not there, but another person.

I did not know if the she had died or gone back to the nursing home, so that following Wednesday when I went to the nursing home she was there and I was very glad to see her. About six months later I was pushing her to our church service and She said, yes I want to go to your church and testify."

I said, "What do you mean?"

She said, "I want to go to your church and testify. The doctors had given me up for dead, but each time you came and prayed for me I began to get better and better."

I was shocked because I had no idea that she was aware that I was in the hospital room praying for her.

Carol

One morning I came downstairs to go to work. My mother said, "Carol is on the porch having one of those things again." Carol suffered with seizures from time to time in which she would go into convulsions and her whole body would shake uncontrollably. I went out on the porch and laid hands on her. I prayed for her in Jesus' name. Before my very eyes I saw this mass — I do not know what it was but it appeared to look like a small dark cloud— lift off her and vanish into the air. She was healed and all right from that moment on.

Toothache

I was on my way to prayer one evening. A woman I knew was riding by; I waved and she stopped. As we were talking she said that she had a severe toothache. She stated that she had taken various medications, but the pain would not go away. I asked her if I could pray for her and she said *yes*. I laid my hands on her head and began to pray for her. When I was finished she said as soon as I touched her she felt a warm sensation come over her body, and the pain of the toothache went away.

Mother Johnson

One Saturday we were in the feeding program at the church and Mother Johnson said she had a bad pain in her back. I asked her if I could pray for her. We went off into a side room and I laid hands on her and began to pray for her in Jesus' name. When I was finished praying for her she said that the pain was gone.

Saint Raphael's

I went to St. Raphael's Hospital to have my teeth extracted. I had nine teeth pulled at once. The dentist told me that once the Novocain wore off I would be in serious pain; therefore, he gave me Tylenol with codeine to take for the pain. I was having second thoughts about taking the medication, but the Novocain was wearing off and I was feeling the pain, so I took one and was feeling all right for a while. I then felt a sharp pain go through my body. I knelt down and said to God, "I don't want to take these Tylenols. I want you to take this pain away." After praying for a while I got up and I did not have the pain anymore. When I went to the dentist for a follow up he asked how many pills I had left. I showed him a full bottle. He asked me why I had so many pills left. My response was, "I just didn't take them."

Lord, You Have Got to Work a Miracle

One day I was at work and I felt a little tight. I decided to do some exercises and felt like I pulled a muscle in the back of my leg. I finished the day at work, but by the time I got home I was in serious pain, so I decided to lie down for a while. When I started to get up I was in such pain that I could barely move. I thought to myself, *what if I can't get up or even walk again?* I had spoken to my nephew and he offered to bring me pain medication. I wondered how I would get them if I could not get up from the bed. I managed to get to the door and leave it open so that my nephew could let himself in. I then hopped to the bed and crawled in. My nephew dropped off the medication and asked if there was anything that he could do for me and I told him *no*. It was the Tuesday before Thanksgiving and I was due to report to Refocus Ministry, my job and the nursing home. My main concern at this point was the nursing home because the minister that was supposed to visit the seniors had surgery and could not make it; therefore, it was up to me to go in his place. I did not want the let the seniors down because they really looked forward to us coming and it was the Thanksgiving holiday.

I prayed to God and said, "You have to work a miracle for me," and he did. That following Wednesday morning I woke up and felt better; however, I was still in pain. I called Refocus ministry and let them know that I was not able to make it and felt bad that I could not go. I then cried out to the Lord and said, "You have to help me because I don't want to let your people down at the nursing home the day before Thanksgiving." I then laid back down and went to sleep. When I woke up, the pain was miraculously gone.

I began to slowly move my leg and felt no pain. I got up and walked around the room and still, no pain. I said to myself, *the true test will be when I try to walk down the stairs*. I went over to the stairs and stepped down and there was no pain. I knew then that God had worked another miracle for me in my life (see Psalm 126:3).

There was another incident when I was in prayer at the church and Deacon Townsend came over to me after prayer and asked if I could pray with him because he was having problems with his shoulder. I looked at him, puzzled, and wondered why he would come to me since I was not a minister or an elder in the church. Deacon Townsend said to me that the Lord spoke to him and told him to come to me for prayer. I prayed with him in Jesus' name And he said to me later that day that the pain went away.

Chapter 4

Demonic Spirits

"**A**nd Jesus rebuked the devil; and he departed out of him: and the child was cured from that very hour." (Matthew 17:18)

"But if I cast out devils by the Spirit of God, then the kingdom of God is come unto you." (Matthew 12:28)

"And he asked him, What is thy name? And he answered, saying, My name is Legion: for we are many." (Mark 5:9)

"But when he had turned about and looked on his disciples, he rebuked Peter, saying, Get thee behind me, Satan: for thou savourest not the things that be of God, but the things that be of men." (Mark 8:33)

"Then certain of the vagabond Jews, exorcists, took upon them to call over them which had evil spirits the name of the LORD Jesus, saying, We adjure you by Jesus whom Paul preacheth. And there were seven sons of one Sceva, a Jew, and chief of the priests, which did so. And the evil spirit answered and said, Jesus I know, and Paul I know; but who are ye? And the man in whom the evil spirit was leaped on them, and overcame them, and prevailed against them, so that they fled out of that house naked and wounded." (Acts 19:13- 16)

Grand Street Ghost

In the early 1970s I was living in the North End of Bridgeport on Goodsell and Main Street. Three people were killed in a particular house on Grand Street that was a block from where I lived. The house was vacant for some time until a man named Oscar moved in. I became friends with Oscar and he would invite me over to his house. I would refuse the invitation, but I never told him why. One day we were outside and he invited me into his house and

I said *yes*. We walked up to his apartment that was located on the second floor. Oscar put the key in the door and we walked inside. There was a tiny doorway that if you walk right in it would lead you into the living room. There we saw the perfect shape of a man that looked like he was made out of cigarette ashes. The man looked and came toward us. When it got a little closer to Oscar and me it turned and went into the kitchen and through the back door, which was shut. We both looked at each other at the same time as if to say, "Did you see that?!"

Rooming House

I was living on Cowles Street in Mrs. Willis' rooming house. It was 12:00 at night and I was in my bed alone in my room when I heard something hit the foot of my bed. I leaned up to see what the noise was when I felt something jump on my leg. It paralyzed me and began to walk up the side of my leg. As I began to move I felt myself break out in a sweat. As this thing moved up a little past my waist, I lifted up my hands and yelled out, "Jesus!" It ran and jumped off the bed. I looked around the room to see if I saw something, but I did not. I was thinking about leaving and going to my mother's house, but because it was so late I decided to stay home.

The next morning, I went by my mother's house and told her what happened. She said that when I gave my life back to Christ the devil was cast out of me and that he was coming to try to possess me. That evening when I saw my pastor, I told him what had happened. He said that my mother was right. He said that the demon was cast out of me and that he was coming back to try and possess me. I asked him why I just called out the name of Jesus. I was new in Christ at the time and I did not know much about God, but my pastor said that it was the Holy Ghost who told me to call out the Name "Jesus." He said that demons tremble at that name!

Little Imps

I was asleep in bed one night when I had this dream. In the dream there were three little imps crawling around my chest. In the dream God told me to go to the kitchen window and tell them to get out. When I woke up I went to the kitchen window, lifted it up and told them to get out of my house.

I went back to bed and about three days later I was asleep in my bed, and felt these little imps running around on my chest. They had little sharp claws that were pricking me. I went to cry out to the Lord and the word came out, "Lourd," as my speech became slurred as if I were drunk. When I gathered myself I called out, "Lord," and they jumped off me. I went to the kitchen window and told them to get out. I was fine from that moment on.

I Called Out, "Jesus."

I was lying in bed one night ready to fall asleep when I felt the atmosphere in the room change. I said, "Uh oh," then all of a sudden I felt this mass come over my head. I could hear it breathing, warm with nasty thoughts and feelings coming over me. I started to call out, "Jesus," but my voice came out low and shaky. I thought to myself, *why are you calling out the name of Jesus as if you are afraid? You know you are not afraid.* When I began to think that thought, the mass disappeared.

I Shook It Off

On October 31, 2014, I had come home from my mother's home going service when I felt something jump on my shoulder. As soon as I felt it, I shook it off. I had been warned to expect an attack from the devil because at my mother's homegoing service nineteen people got saved.

Legion

I was in church one Sunday morning and this man came in. He was kind of bummy and raggedy looking and I wanted to shake his hand to make him feel welcomed, as we were taught to do. Something was telling me not to, but I went and shook his hand anyway. When I shook his hand this spirit came over me, and my mouth started to twist and I felt like I was going to have a stroke. I started to walk around and rebuke that spirit and call on Jesus and after about three minutes I shook that spirit off me.

Witnessing in P.T. Barnum Apartments

One Saturday a group of us went to P.T. Barnum Apartments to witness to lost souls. When we arrived there we walked around for a while handing out tracts, praying and talking with people. Then we went into the courtyard. It was like we were at a drug flea market. There were people buying and selling drugs, people drinking and smoking and laughing. There were women walking around looking for someone to sell their bodies to. There was even one guy under the stairs with a needle in his arm pit. It was four of us together that day and we decided to pray right on the spot. We joined hands and began to pray earnestly for the people. We were not yelling and screaming; we just prayed. I had my eyes closed as we prayed. We did not pray a very long time, but all I know is when we stopped praying I opened my eyes and everyone was gone. We looked at each other and said, "Where did all those people go?" It was truly amazing what happened that day!

"Our weapons of warfare are not carnal; but mighty through God to the pulling down of strongholds." 2 Corinthians 10:4.

What a mighty God we serve!

Chapter 5

What People Have Spoken To Me Concerning My Walk With God

"He saith unto them, But whom say ye that I am? And Simon Peter answered and said, Thou art the Christ, the Son of the living God. And Jesus answered and said unto him, Blessed art thou, Simon Barjona: for flesh and blood hath not revealed it unto thee, but my Father which is in heaven." (Matthew 16:15-17)

"I beseech you therefore, brethren, by the mercies of God, that ye present your bodies a living sacrifice, holy, acceptable unto God, which is your reasonable service. And be not conformed to this world: but be ye transformed by the renewing of your mind, that ye may prove what is that good, and acceptable, and perfect, will of God." (Romans 12:1-2)

"Ye are our epistle written in our hearts, known and read of all men" (2 Corinthians 3:2)

A Holy Man of God

One evening I was at Bridgeport Manor and a woman motioned me to come over to her. I looked around to see who she was talking to and she pointed to me. I went over to her and she said that she had been working at the nursing home for a very long time. She said that she was ready to go and work for another nursing home. However, she said that she had something to say to me and that she did not know why she was telling me this. She said, "I know that you are a holy man of God. Lots of men say they are men of God, but they are not. I know that you are a holy man of God." She said that God showed me to her in a dream preaching in a church and that I was holy. I did not know this woman at all and even though she told me her name. To this day I cannot remember her name or what she looks like.

Pray for Me

One day I was walking down Stratford Avenue in Bridgeport. A guy came up behind me and tapped me on my shoulder and said, "Pray for me." I looked at him as if to say, "Who are you?"

He said to me, "I know you. I remember when you used to walk up and down these streets getting high, and now you walk around as if it doesn't bother you."

I said, "It doesn't. What God has done for me, he can do it for you, also." I then began to pray with him (see St. John 17:15).

You Have a Testimony

I was walking down Stratford Avenue, near Tiffany's where I got saved that night. I was singing in my spirit this song, I don't quite remember who the artist is but it went like this,

"When I look back over my life and I think things over, I can truly say that I've been blessed, I have a testimony. Testimony, testimony, testimony."

There was this guy coming up the street and I believe his name was Harold. Lots of people think he is crazy or a little off because he always walks around with this big old Bible under his arm. When he saw me he looked at me and smiled and said, "You have a testimony," it's almost like we were one in the spirit. Right there I knew he was not crazy as some people think because he knew what I was singing in my spirit. I told him that I was just singing that song to myself.

I See Jesus in You

One Sunday morning it was right after service a young woman looked at me and started laughing and kept on laughing. She said, "I see Jesus in you. I see Jesus in you."

You Have No Idea

I was in the feeding program at our church one day and this woman said to me, "You have no idea how many people are watching you. I remember when you lived on

Cowles Street." The Bible says that we are to be living epistles written and read among men (2 Corinthians 3:2).